NOTE: There are dozens of wonderful poetry books available today. Select those most appropriate for your class. This bibliography lists some of our favorites.

Bibliography of Poetry Books

A Light in the Attic by Shel Silverstein; Harper & Row, 1981.

Cricket Songs translated by Harry Behn; Harcourt, Brace, and World Inc., 1964 (Haiku).

don't tell the scarecrow by Issa, et al.; Four Winds Press, 1969 (Haiku).

Feathered Ones and Furry by Aileen Fisher; Thomas Y. Crowell,1971.

Hiawatha by Henry Wadsworth Longfellow; Dial Books for Young Readers, 1983.

Knock At a Star by X. J. Kennedy & Dorothy M. Kennedy; Little, Brown & Company, 1982.

Mother Goose by Michael Hague; Holt, Rinehart and Winston, 1984.

My Own Rhythm by Ann Atwood; Charles Scribner's Sons, 1973 (Haiku).

Oh, A-Hunting We Will Go by John Langstaff; Atheneum, 1974 (Couplets).

Paul Revere's Ride by Henry Wadsworth Longfellow; Greenwillow Books, 1978.

Pigericks by Arnold Lobel;Harper & Row, 1983 (Limericks).

Poetry on Wheels selected by Lee Bennett Hopkins; Garrard Publishing Company, 1974.

Ring of Earth by Jane Yolen; Harcourt Brace Jovanovich, 1986.

Stopping By the Woods on a Snowy Evening by Robert Frost; E. P. Dutton, 1978.

The Moon's the North Wind's Cooky selected by Susan Russo; Lothrop, Lee & Shepard Company, 1979.

The Oxford Book of Children's Verse in America edited by Donald Hall; Oxford University Press, 1985.

The Random House Book of Poetry for Children selected by Jack Prelutsky; Random House, 1983.

Think of Shadows by Lillian Moore; Atheneum, 1980.

Writing Poetry With Children

The purpose of *Writing Poetry With Children* is not to attempt to turn out a nation of young poets. Its goal is to provide opportunities for children to experience and explore the wonder that poetry can provide. Children need to hear and use the rich language, the rhythm, and the expression of feelings that make a poem.

Your students will need to experience poetry in many ways before starting to write on their own. You will find suggestions for using poetry in various areas of your curriculum on page 4. The more poems children have heard, the easier your task will be when you start teaching poetry writing skills.

Poetry is difficult to write. Not all children will be able to create excellent poems. But they can all benefit by the opportunity to explore the various forms and to discover if they enjoy writing it or not.

This resource book attempts to provide the busy teacher with the information and the guidance to make poetry writing successful and pleasurable for both teacher and student. Select the forms of verse you feel are appropriate for your grade level. Don't expect first efforts to always be successful. A simple form such as a couplet may require minimal guidance with your class. More complicated forms such as limericks or blank verse can require many guided lessons before your students are ready to try on their own. Encourage students as they attempt the various forms, but don't give false praise. Regardless of the type of poem, you want your students to do their best.

Provide opportunities for children to share their poems with each other. This can be as simple as reading a poem to the person next to them or as complicated as making a book of poems to place in the classroom library. Pages 55 to 63 have a variety of ways to display and share original poems.

Reading and writing poetry should be an enjoyable experience for both teacher and students. I hope the ideas and activities provided in *Writing Poetry With Children* help make it a pleasure for you both.

3

Using Poetry as a Teaching Tool

Use your favorite poems to add interest to daily skills practice in a variety of academic areas. Poetry can be used to:

Practice memory skills

Develop concepts

Recall information

Develop a richer vocabulary

Search for opposites, rhyming words, synonyms, etc.

Find the nouns, verbs, adjectives, etc.

Practice counting skills

Sequence

Use dictionary and thesaurus

Find metaphors and similes

Look for alliteration

Compare and contrast

- two poems on the same topic

- two poems in the same/different style

- different poems by the same poet

4

Steps to Follow in Writing Poetry With Children

Before you write:
Read to your class many poems written in the style you intend to practice. This gives them an opportunity to become familiar with the rhythm, rhyming pattern, etc. of the specific poetry form before they attempt to write it themselves.

Writing:
Guide your students through their first writing experiences with the poetry style before they attempt it on their own.

Select a topic of interest to your students.

Brainstorm together to create lists of ideas and words or phrases to use when writing the poem.

Do initial writing experiences together. With each experience have your students do more of the steps independently.

When you feel your students are ready, have them do entire poems on their own. Allow time for older students to do re-writing. This extra time will result in better poetry.

Use the children's own work to find examples of good use of language, rhyme, etc. to share with the class. This is especially helpful for students who are hesitant to write.

Share finished results:
Provide places and opportunities for students to reread their own poems and to share the poems of their classmates.

Remember — Go through the poetry form step-by-step with your students before requiring them to write on their own. The more comfortable they are with the poetry form, the better the results will be. Allow re-writing time for older and more able students. Re-writing can transform an ordinary poem into something special.

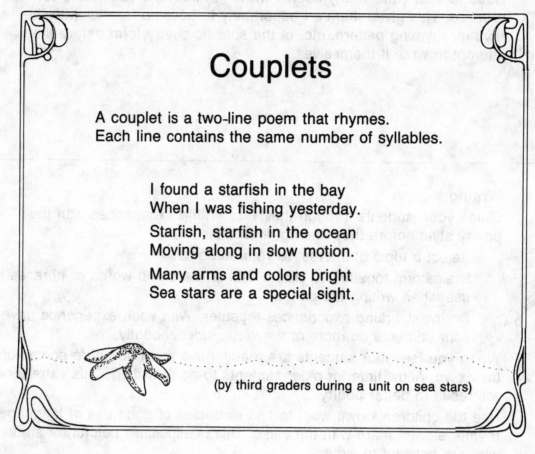

Couplets

A couplet is a two-line poem that rhymes.
Each line contains the same number of syllables.

I found a starfish in the bay
When I was fishing yesterday.

Starfish, starfish in the ocean
Moving along in slow motion.

Many arms and colors bright
Sea stars are a special sight.

(by third graders during a unit on sea stars)

Variations:

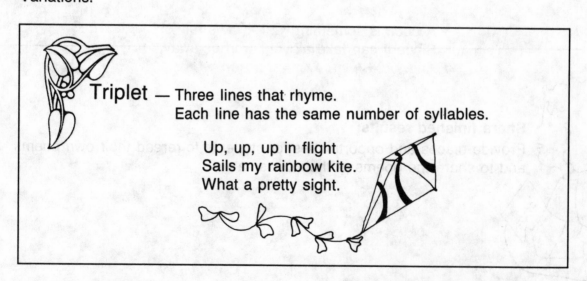

Triplet — Three lines that rhyme.
Each line has the same number of syllables.

Up, up, up in flight
Sails my rainbow kite.
What a pretty sight.

 Writing Poetry With Children

NOTE: These quatrains are by Danielle Wall, sixth grade.

Quatrain — Four lines with several possible rhyming patterns.

AABB — lines 1 and 2 rhyme, lines 3 and 4 rhyme

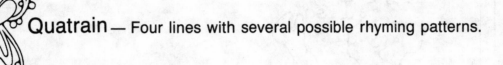

Birthday parties are colorful, surprising affairs,
With presents of dolls and cute teddy bears.
After the presents come cake and ice cream.
The party girl certainly feels like a queen.

ABAB — lines 1 and 3 rhyme, lines 2 and 4 rhyme

The wind is a creature with glistening wings,
Who flits about and gossips with the deer.
She is more playful, though, in the middle of Spring,
When she blows nice, warm breezes against my ear.

ABCB — lines 2 and 4 rhyme, lines 1 and 3 do not rhyme

A book is something you always rely on,
Since it can take all your worries away,
And send you off on an adventurous journey,
Or a little picnic on a bright, sunny day.

ABBA — lines 1 and 4 rhyme, lines 2 and 3 rhyme

A museum is a place where time disappears,
You may be a young pirate sailing the ocean waves,
Or a brave Spanish explorer in search of golden caves,
But when you leave the museum, time reappears.

Writing Poetry With Children

Steps for Writing Couplets

In the beginning, do several verses together. Younger students will need more practice than older or more able students. Read couplets aloud to your class to demonstrate the rhyming pattern.

- Level I   Guide students through all the steps.
             (See Sample A.)

> 1. Provide the first sentence.
> 2. List rhyming words.
> 3. Do second lines together.

- Level II   Guide students through steps one
             and two.
             Students do step three independently.
             (See Sample B.)

- Level III Students do all the steps
             independently.

Sample A

Guide students through all steps.

1. Select a topic of interest to your students.

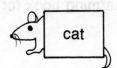

   Provide the first sentence. The complexity of the sentence will depend on the specific needs of your class.

   I saw a black cat...
   or
   Quietly staring, the cat...

2. Brainstorm to create a list of words rhyming with the topic. (This is a great time to use a dictionary or thesaurus if you have students in grades three or higher.)

hat	fat	sat
pat	mat	vat
bat	rat	flat

3. The class creates the second line of the couplet together.

   I saw a black cat
   Asleep on the mat.
   I saw a black cat
   That was very fat.
   I saw a black cat
   Chasing a rat.

   Quietly staring, the cat
   Was mesmerized by a bat.
   Quietly staring, the cat
   Settled down on her mat.
   Quietly staring, the cat
   Purred as I gave her a pat.

You may choose to have your students copy their favorite couplets and illustrate them to put into a class book.

cut

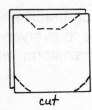
draw

fold

staple

9

Guide students through steps one and two. They do step three independently.

Read couplets aloud to demonstrate the rhyming pattern. (*Oh, A-Hunting We Will Go* by John Langstaff is a charming book for younger students illustrating the couplet form.)

1. Select a topic.

fox

2. Provide the first sentence.

I heard of a fox...

or

A mysterious fox...

3. Brainstorm to create a list of words that rhymes with the topic.

box	clocks	rocks
docks	socks	walks
blocks	locks	hawks
chicken pox		

4. Have your students create the second lines independently.

I heard of a fox
Who was in a box.

A mysterious fox
Hides from big hawks.

I heard of a fox
Who is afraid of rocks.

A mysterious fox
Took lonely walks.

I heard of a fox
Who had chicken pox.

A mysterious fox
Howls when he talks.

I heard of a fox
Who played with his blocks.

A mysterious fox
Jumped over rocks.

(by a class of first graders)

Have each child copy his/her poem neatly and illustrate it.

When you feel your class has had sufficient group practice, have them write a couplet independently. You may assign a topic to everyone (pages 13-15 have sample topics for independent writing) or brainstorm with your class to develop a list of possible topics.

NOTE: Reproduce these directions for your students to follow in writing couplets. (You may want to put the directions on a chart to display in your classroom.)

Write a Couplet

Follow these directions:

1. **Think about your topic. Decide what you want to say about it in your poem.**

    Write your first sentence.

2. **Make a list of words that rhymes with the last word in your sentence.**

3. **Write your second sentence.**

    Does it rhyme with the first line?

    Does it have the same number of syllables?

Write a Couplet

_____
(Title)

Write your first sentence here.

_____

_____

_____

Make a list of words that rhymes with the last word of your sentence.

_____   _____

_____   _____

Write your second sentence here.

_____

_____

_____

Copy your poem here. Make a picture to illustrate the poem.

_____

_____

_____

_____

_____

_____

_____

_____

NOTE: Reproduce this sheet to use when writing a couplet (or other poem) about the sun.

The Sun

by _____

Birds

by _____

Rain

by _____

_____

_____

_____

_____

_____

_____

_____

_____

_____

_____

_____

_____

_____

_____

_____

_____

_____

_____

Remember — Go through the poetry form step-by-step with your students before requiring them to write on their own. The more comfortable they are with the poetry form, the better the results will be. Allow re-writing time for older and more able students. Re-writing can transform an ordinary poem into something special.

Cinquain

A cinquain does not rhyme. It follows a pattern of five lines containing 22 syllables.

(You may choose to ignore an exact syllable count when working with primary students or less-able intermediate level students.)

> Line 1 — two syllables
> Line 2 — four syllables
> Line 3 — six syllables
> Line 4 — eight syllables
> Line 5 — two syllables

A form that is successful with many students relies on word count rather than a strict adherence to syllable count.

> Line 1 — one word (title)
> Line 2 — two words (describe the title)
> Line 3 — three words (describe an action)
> Line 4 — four words (describe a feeling)
> Line 5 — one word (refer back to the title)

Crocodile
Has teeth
Scaring his enemies
Full after his meal
Sleepy
(by a second grader)

Owl
Swift, ferocious
Watches for food
Soaring through the night
Hunter
(by a third grader)

Hamsters
Furry creatures
Twitching little noses,
Loving, cozy, fluffy cotton
Cuddly
(by a sixth grader)

Otter
Gentle baby
Dives for food
Loves the cool water
Otter
(by a second grader)

Writing Poetry With Children

Steps for Writing a Cinquain

In the beginning, do several verses together. Younger students will need more practice than older or more able students. Read cinquains aloud to your class to demonstrate the pattern.

- **Level I** Guide students through all the steps.
  (See Sample A.)

  1. Provide the topic.
  2. For each succeeding step:
     Brainstorm vocabulary and ideas for each line.
  3. Write each line together using the ideas developed in step 2.

- **Level II** Guide students through steps one and two.
  They do step three independently.
  (See Sample B.)

- **Level III** Students do all the steps independently.

Sample A

Guide students through all steps.

1. Select a topic of interest to your students.
   (Decide if you are going to use the "word" form or the "syllable" form.
   This example uses the "word" form.)
   Write the title on the chalkboard or a chart.

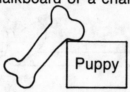

Puppy

2. Brainstorm to develop a list of words that describes the title.

soft	furry	floppy ears
curly tail	happy tail	black spots

3. Brainstorm to develop a list of three-word phrases that describes an action relating to the topic.

runs in circles	chasing my cat	digging for bones
wiggles in sleep	fetching a stick	follows me home

4. Brainstorm to develop a list of four-word phrases that describes a feeling experienced by or about the topic.

happy to see me	eager to play again
dreaming of lost bones	protecting his back yard
chasing his own tail	hungry for a snack

5. Brainstorm to develop a list of words that refers back to the title.

dog	pet	friend
collie	companion	pal

6. The class decides on a word or phrase for each line of the cinquain.

Puppy	Puppy
Happy tail	Soft, furry
Follows me home	Wiggles in sleep
Eager to play again	Dreaming of lost bones
Pal	Pet

You may select students to copy the class cinquain and illustrate it. Put these poems into a class poetry book.

  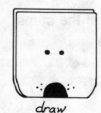 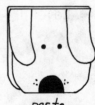 

cut   draw   cut ears   paste   fold + staple

Writing Poetry With Children

Sample B

Guide students through steps one to five. They do step six independently.

1. Select a topic of interest to your students. (This sample uses "syllable" form.) Encourage your students to come up with an idea first. Then worry about the correct number of syllables.

    List the title on the chalkboard.

     Dragon

2. Brainstorm to develop a list of four-syllable words or phrases about a topic.

    swiftly flying   mythical beast

3. Brainstorm to develop a list of six-syllable phrases about the topic.

    searching the land below
    shrieking as he attacks
    seeking food for dinner
    following the brave knight

4. Brainstorm to develop a list of eight-syllable phrases about the topic.

    soaring over the mountain tops
    shadow darkens the land below
    waiting in anticipation
    silent death dropping from the sky

5. Brainstorm to create a list of two-syllable words or phrases that refers back to the title.

    hungry   danger   fable
    beast   farewell   battle

6. Students create their own cinquain using the lists created by the class.

    Dragon   Dragon
    Swiftly flying   Mythical beast
    Searching the land below   Following the brave knight
    Waiting in anticipation   Silent death dropping from the sky
    Hungry   Battle

When you feel your class has had sufficient group practice, have them write independent cinquains. You may assign a topic to everyone (pages 22-24 have sample topics for independent writing) or brainstorm with your class to develop a list of possible topics.

NOTE: Reproduce these directions for your students to follow in writing a cinquain using the "counted word" form. (You may want to put the directions on a chart to display in your classroom.)

Write a Cinquain

Follow these steps:

1. Decide on your one-word title.

2. Think of two-word phrases that describe your topic. Select the phrase you like best.

3. Think of three-word phrases that describe an action relating to your topic. Choose the phrase you like best.

4. Think of four-word phrases that describe a feeling relating to your topic. Choose the phrase you like best.

5. Think of one word that refers back to your topic.

Write a Cinquain

1. Decide on your one-word title. Write it here.

   _____

2. Think of two-word phrases that describe your topic. Write the best phrase here.

   _____ _____

   _____ _____

3. Think of three-word phrases that tell something the topic can do. Write the phrase you like best here.

   _____

   _____

   _____

4. Think of four-word phrases that describe a feeling about your topic. Write the phrase you like best here.

   _____

   _____

   _____

5. Think of one word that refers back to your title. Write it here.

   _____

6. Copy your cinquain here.

   _____

   _____

   _____

   _____

Butterfly

by _____

Bubbles

by _____

_____

_____

_____

_____

_____

_____

_____

_____

_____

_____

_____

_____

_____

A Space Ship

by _____

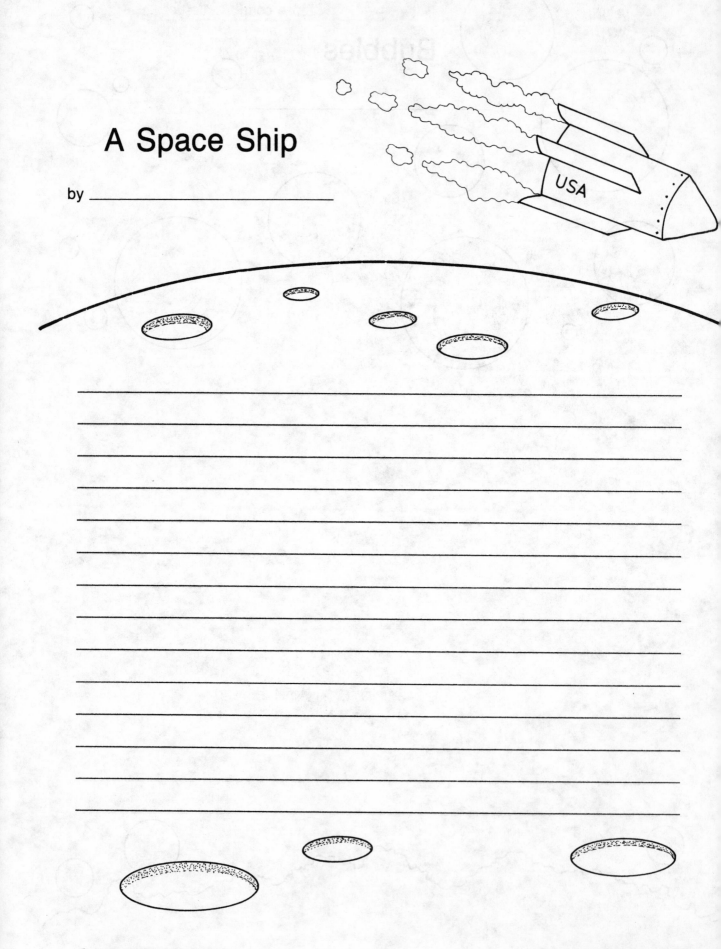

Remember — Go through the poetry form step-by-step with your students before requiring them to write on their own. The more comfortable they are with the poetry form, the better the results will be. Allow re-writing time for older and more able students. Re-writing can transform an ordinary poem into something special.

Haiku

A haiku poem consists of seventeen unrhymed syllables organized into three lines.

> Line 1 — five syllables
> Line 2 — seven syllables
> Line 3 — five syllables

Most haiku poems refer to some element of nature. They express a moment of beauty which keeps you thinking or feeling.

Younger students may be unable to handle an exact measure of seventeen syllables, but many can express a feeling within the short one sentence format. In the beginning (for any grade level), it can be helpful to provide a simple guide that delineates the elements of the verse. For example:

> where it happens............On my backyard fence
> what is happening..........a cat sings his lonely song
> when it occurs...............each hot summer night.

The most important thing to remember is that the thought should come first. Then consider adjusting the syllable count.

The hungry frog
resting on a lily pad
dreams of careless flies.

Tiny hummingbirds
dart from flower to flower.
Rainbows in motion.

Gentle raindrops fall.
Reflected in the puddles,
thirsty flowers drink.

In freezing weather,
Little snowflakes start falling.
Catch them on your tongue.

When winter arrives
trees change into dark shadows
in my neighbor's yard.

One sparkling spring day
I saw a tiny spider
spin a web of silk.

Writing Poetry With Children

Steps for Writing a Haiku

Read many examples from the works of Japanese masters such as Basho, Buson, or Bondo aloud to your students to help them understand the pattern and feelings expressed in the haiku verse form.

Having objects from nature or pictures of seasonal themes can be helpful in stimulating writing ideas. Walks outside to observe nature and the seasons first hand are helpful also.

In the beginning, do several verses together. Remind children to begin with the thought. Adjust syllables later.

- Level I Guide students through all of the steps together.
  (See Sample A.)

  1. Provide the topic.

  2. Brainstorm to create a list of phrases that tells where the action is occurring.

  3. Brainstorm to create a list of phrases that tells what is happening.

  4. Brainstorm to create a list of phrases that tells when it occurred.

  5. Write a sentence together using one phrase from each list.

  6. Adjust the syllable count in each phrase (or in the total poem).

  With younger or less able students, you may want to accept the lovely word picture created by the group without worrying about an exact syllable count.

- Level II Guide students through steps one, two, three, and four. They do steps five and six independently.

- Level III Children do all steps independently.

Follow these steps with children ready to try to write a traditional haiku poem.

> That fat old bull-frog   Sweet spring shower...
> Sat there staring   Enough to wet the
>   back at me   tiny shells
> With a sour face.   On this little beach
>
>   Issa   Buson

- **Level I**   Guide students through all of the steps together.
          (See Sample B.)

  1. Provide the topic. (You may want to have a picture or the actual item present to help stimulate ideas.)
  2. Brainstorm to create a list of phrases or sentences about the topic.
  3. Write a basic sentence together using the ideas developed in step 2.
  4. Adjust the syllables and placement of phrase to fit the correct haiku pattern.

- **Level II**   Guide students through steps one and two. Have them do steps three and four independently. Some children will still need individual help in doing step four.

- **Level III**   Children do all steps independently.

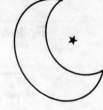

1. Select an object from nature or a photograph of a seasonal scene to stimulate ideas. Discuss the elements present in the picture.

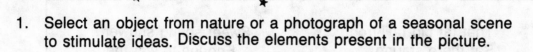

Example — a picture of waves breaking on a beach in the moonlight.

2. Brainstorm to create lists of words or phrases that tell where the action is occurring.

      beach   at the ocean
      sea   along the shoreline

3. Brainstorm to create lists of phrases that tell what is happening.

      moonlight is shining
      restless waves are moving in and out
      whitecaps show in the moonlight
      tide is coming in

4. Brainstorm to create lists of phrases that tell when it is happening

      in the summer   at night
      in the moonlight   after the sun sets
      about midnight   each year

5. Write a phrase for each word using the ideas developed in steps two through four.

      Where — at the beach where the moon is shining
      What — the restless waves are moving in and out
      When — on summer nights

6. Adjust the syllables and words to fit the haiku pattern.

      On the moonlit beach
        restless waves move endlessly...
        Quiet summer night.

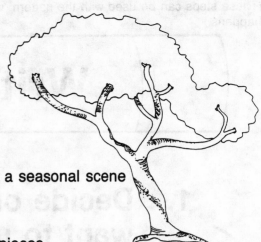

Sample B

1. Select an object from nature or a photograph of a seasonal scene to stimulate ideas.

> Example — Have children touch pieces
> of bark from an oak tree.

2. Brainstorm to create a list of words or phrases that describes how the object looks, feels, etc., or how you feel about the object.

brown	feels rough in my hand
deep cracks	children touch the bark
curious	bark from an old tree
ancient	a strange feeling

3. Write a sentence using the ideas developed in step two.

> The bark from the ancient oak felt rough in the curious child's hands.

4. Adjust the syllables and words to fit the haiku pattern.

> 5 syllables — Oh, ancient oak tree
> 7 syllables — how strange your rugged bark felt
> 5 syllables — to curious hands.

Write a Haiku

1. **Decide on your topic. (You may want to use a picture or an object to help get you started.)**

2. **Make a list of phrases that tells where the action is occurring.**

3. **Make a list of phrases that tells what is happening.**

4. **Make a list of phrases that tells when the action is taking place.**

5. **Write a haiku using your favorite phrase from each list.**

6. **Make changes until you have your seventeen syllables.**

 Writing Poetry With Children

Write a Haiku

1. **Decide on your topic. (You may use a picture or object to help you get started.)**

2. **Write several phrases or sentences describing an action or feeling about your topic. Remember to refer to nature or the season.**

3. **Choose the phrases or sentence that you like the best. Work to make them fit the correct haiku form.**

    5 syllables
    7 syllables
    5 syllables

NOTE: You may reproduce this form for students to use when writing haiku following a "where, what, when" pattern.

Write a Haiku

1. Select a topic. (You may want to look at an object or a picture to help you get started.) Write your topic here.

    _____

2. Think about your topic. Write words or phrases that tell where action could be occurring.

    _____

    _____

    _____

3. Write words or phrases that tell what could be happening.

    _____

    _____

    _____

4. Write words or phrases that tell when it could be happening.

    _____

    _____

    _____

5. Write a phrase for each word using the ideas you have written.

    Where _____

    What _____

    When _____

6. Adjust the syllables and words to fit the haiku pattern. Write your haiku here.

    _____

    _____

    _____

    _____

Write a Haiku

1. Select a topic. (You may want to use an object or picture to help you get started.) Write your topic here.

    _____

2. Think about your topic. Write a list of words or phrases that describes the object or picture and words or phrases that tell how you feel about it.

    _____

    _____

    _____

3. Write a sentence using the ideas you wrote in step two. Write your sentence here.

    _____

    _____

    _____

4. Adjust the syllables and words to fit the haiku pattern. Write your haiku here.

    _____

    5 syllables _____

    7 syllables _____

    5 syllables _____

The Willow Tree

by _____

_____

_____

_____

_____

_____

_____

_____

_____

_____

_____

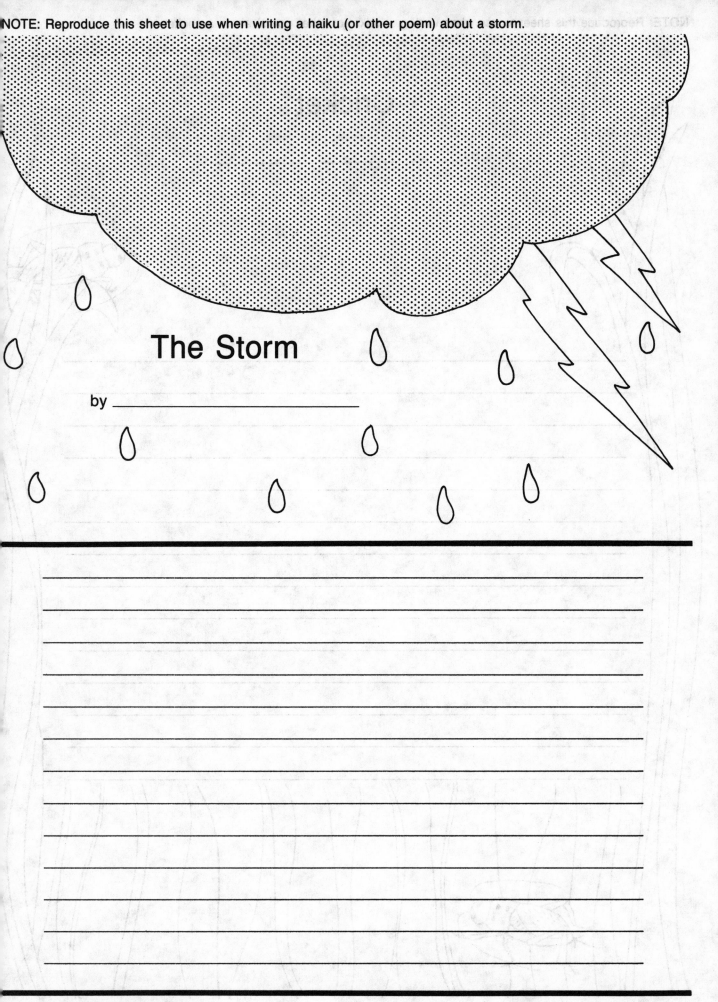

The Storm

by _____

Cricket

by _____

Remember — Go through the poetry form step-by-step with your students before requiring them to write on their own. The more comfortable they are with the poetry form, the better the results will be. Allow re-writing time for older and more able students. Re-writing can transform an ordinary poem into something special.

Limericks

A limerick is an amusing verse of five lines. There are three long lines which rhyme and two short lines that rhyme.

Line 1 _____ a
Line 2 _____ a
    Line 3 _____ b
    Line 4 _____ b
Line 5 _____ a

There once was a musical king
Who suddenly started to sing.
    The birds in the sky
    All started to fly
Nearer that talented king.

There once was a lass from Bombay
Who was heard to angrily say
    "When my husband — the rat
    Rudely sat on my cat,
I instantly chased him away!"

Ogg, the fire-breathing dragon
Was sad cause his tail wasn't waggin'.
    So his fire-breathing friends
    Tied springs to the ends.
Now that dragon is waggin'and braggin'.

by Leslie Tryon

The limerick form is too difficult for primary students. Intermediate students will need considerable guidance in the beginning.

37 Writing Poetry With Children

NOTE: Some students may never be able to do limericks alone. Provide these students with an opportunity to work with a partner or in a small group.

Steps for Writing Limericks

In the beginning, do several verses together. Read limericks aloud to your class to demonstrate the limerick rhythm and rhyming pattern. (Two sources you might use are *The Book of Nonsense* by Edward Lear and *The Book of Pigericks* by Arnold Lobel.)

- Level I   Guide students through all the steps. (See Sample A.)

    1. Provide line one, two, and five.

    2. Brainstorm ideas for short lines three and four. List these ideas on the chalkboard.

    3. Students decide which of these ideas they like best. They then work together to turn the phrases into two lines that rhyme.

- Level II   Guide students through lines one, two, and five. You may want to follow a simple form to help get them started. For example:

    ☆ There once was a ____ named ____
    ☆ Who _____
    _____
    _____
    ☆ That _____ named _____.

    Students write lines three and four independently. (Some of your students will need individual help at this point.) (See Sample B.)

- Level III   Students do all the steps independently.

38

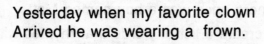

1. Provide lines one, two, and five.

> Yesterday when my favorite clown
> Arrived he was wearing a frown.
> _____
> _____
>
> I'm getting a new job in town.

2. Brainstorm to create a list of possible ideas to fit into lines three and four.

> tired of falling
> slip on a peel
> pie in the face
> laughed at every day
> stuffed in a car
> going from place to place

3. Select the line or lines your students like best. Work with the words to form two short rhyming sentences.

> Yesterday when my favorite clown
> Arrived he was wearing a frown.
>   "I'm tired of the way
>   I'm laughed at each day.
> I'm getting a new job in town."

> Yesterday when my favorite clown
> Arrived he was wearing a frown.
>   "No more pies in the face.
>   It's just a rat race.
> I'm getting a new job in town."

Sample B

1. Guide your students through lines one, two, and five.

   Line 1 — Brainstorm to complete the sentence:
   There once was a_____ named _____.

   > There once was a boy named Matt

   Brainstorm to create a list of words that rhymes with the final word in line one.

hat	bat	sat	drat
cat	rat	flat	scat

   Line 2 — Brainstorm to complete a sentence that tells what was done.

   > Who found something strange in his hat.
   > Whose pet was a big striped cat.
   > Who discovered his bike tire was flat.

   Have your students decide which line they prefer.

   > There once was a boy named Matt
   > Who found something strange in his hat.

   Line 5 — At this point you may complete a line that refers back to line one.

   > Astonished that boy named Matt.

   Or wait until the two short lines have been written so the final line closes the limerick more creatively.

2. Children create their own short couplets for lines three and four.

3. Have each child copy the lines created together, add their individual couplets for lines three and four, and illustrate their limericks.

> There once was a boy named Matt
> Who found something strange in his hat.
>   Six pennies, some slime,
>   And a story in rhyme.
> Astonished that boy named Matt.

When you feel your class has had sufficient group practice, have them write limericks independently. You may assign a topic to everyone (pages 43-45 have sample topics for independent writing) or brainstorm with your class to develop a list of possible topics.

Writing Poetry With Children

Write a Limerick

Line 1 _____ a
Line 2 _____ a
Line 3 _____ b
Line 4 _____ b
Line 5 _____ a

1. **Choose the name of the person, place, or thing your limerick is going to be about.**

2. **Create your first line. (You may want to follow the pattern "There was a _____ named _____." or "There once was a _____ from _____."**

   Make a list of words that rhymes with the last word in your first line.

3. **Think of a second line that rhymes with your first line.**

4. **Write two short lines that rhyme which tell something about your topic.**

5. **Now think of a final line that rhymes with your first line. (You may want to repeat part of your first line following the pattern "That _____ named _____." or "That _____ from _____."**

6. **Write your whole limerick on a sheet of paper. Illustrate it.**

Write a Limerick

1. Choose the name of the person, place or thing your limerick is about. Write it here.

2. Think about your first line. Write it here.

    _____

    Make a list of words that rhymes with the last word in your first line.

    _____   _____

    _____   _____

3. Think of a second line. Remember to make it rhyme with line one. Write it here.

    _____

4. Write two short sentences that tell about your topic. (Remember that they have to rhyme with each other.)

    _____

    _____

    _____

5. Write your final line. It must rhyme with lines one and two. (You may want to repeat part of line one.)

    _____

6. Write your whole limerick here.

    Line 1 — _____

    Line 2 — _____

    Line 3 — _____

    Line 4 — _____

    Line 5 — _____

Note: Reproduce this sheet to use when writing a limerick (or other poem) about a bat.

Bat

by _____

_____
_____
_____
_____
_____
_____
_____
_____
_____
_____
_____
_____
_____
_____

NOTE: Reproduce this sheet to use when writing a limerick (or other poem) about an old man with a beard.

An Old Man With a Beard

by _____

NOTE: Reproduce this sheet to use when writing a limerick (or other poem) about a knight.

The Knight

by _____

_____
_____
_____
_____
_____
_____
_____
_____
_____
_____
_____

45

Poetry Forms for Fun

Sometimes it is fun to play with words in unusual ways to create a poem. Shape and alphabet poems provide an opportunity for this type of experience.

Steps in writing a shape poem:

(See Sample A.)

1. Select an object. Simple shapes work best.

2. List descriptive words and phrases about the object. Select the best ones and arrange them so they have a pleasing sound.

3. Draw the basic outline of the shape with black crayon or marking pen. Place a sheet of plain paper (ditto or typing) over the drawing. Fasten the pages together with a paper clip.

4. Write the words or phrases following the shape of the object to create the "shape" poem. Remove the top sheet of paper to see the completed poem.

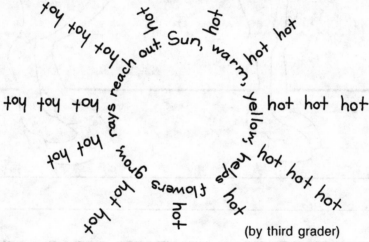

(by third grader)

Steps in writing an alphabet poem:

(See Sample B.)

1. Select a word.

2. List as many words as you can that describe or relate to the word. (This can lead to good practice with a dictionary or thesaurus.)

3. Write the word vertically.
    Select one word from your list that starts with each letter of the word.
    Your goal is to create a descriptive phrase or sentence about the word.

4. Illustrate the poem.

dashing
over
ground

lovely
even
after
falling

   Writing Poetry With Children

kitten

1. Select a topic.

2. Brainstorm to list words or phrases about the topic.

   small   wiggly tail
   purrs   sensitive whiskers
   pink tongue   chases birds and mice
   soft fur   hides in a flower pot
   etc.   etc.

3. Have students choose the words and phrases they like best and arrange them to create a pleasing sound.

   purring kitten cleans her soft fur with a small pink tongue,
   hides in a flower pot on hot days, watches the birds while
   only her tail moves

4. Students draw the outline of a kitten using black crayon or marking pen. Clip a sheet of white paper (ditto or typing) over the drawing. They then write their words and phrases following the shape of their pictures.

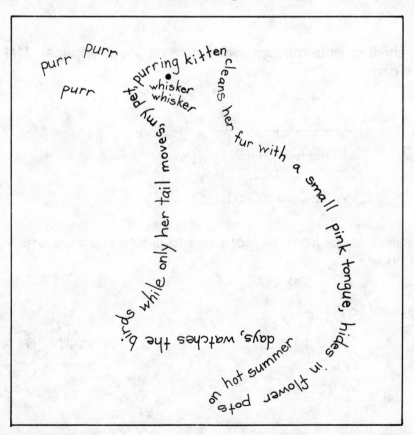

5. Have children paste their poems to sheets of colored paper (to make a frame).

Sample B

1. Choose a word.

> snow

2. Brainstorm to make a list of words about snow. The words must begin with the letters in snow.

soft	new	over	white
slushy	nestle	out	winter
smooth	nice	of	wonderful
sparkling	noiseless	ooze	wild

3. Have children write the topic word down a sheet of paper. Make the letters dark.

s _____

n _____

o _____

w _____

4. Now select words from the word lists to create a phrase or sentence about snow.

softly
nestles
over
winter

Writing Poetry With Children

Write a Shape Poem

1. Choose a topic (an animal, object, or plant). Write it here.

2. Make a list of words or phrases that tells about your topic.

3. Choose the words and phrases you like best and arrange them to create a pleasing sound.

4. Get a sheet of paper. Draw an outline of your topic with black crayon or a marking pen. Clip a sheet of thin white paper over your drawing. Write your words and phrases following the outline you drew.

5. Paste your shape poem to a sheet of colored paper (to make a frame).

Aa　Bb　Cc　Dd　Ee　Ff　Gg　Hh　Ii　Jj　Kk　Ll

Write an Alphabet Poem

Bb

1. Choose a word. Write it here.

Cc

2. Think of as many words as you can that describe the word you picked. The words should all begin with one of the letters in the word you chose. (You may need to use your dictionary or thesaurus.)

Dd

Ee

Ff

Gg

_____　_____　_____

_____　_____　_____

_____　_____　_____

_____　_____　_____

Hh

3. Write your word *down* this paper. Make the letters dark. Pick some of the words from your list. Use them to form a phrase or sentence. Write one word by each letter.

Ii

_____

Jj

_____

_____

Kk

_____

_____

Ll

_____

_____

Mm

_____

_____

Nn

4. You may copy your alphabet poem on a sheet of good paper and illustrate it.

50

Oo　Pp　Qq　Rr　Ss　Tt　Uu　Vv　Ww　Xx　Yy

NOTE: After your students have been exposed to a variety of poetry forms, provide opportunities for practice using their favorite forms.

More Poetry Writing Ideas

1. Re-write nursery rhymes.

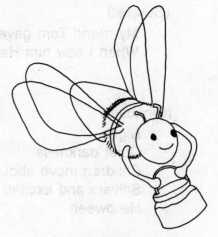

Flicker, flicker little light
Shining brightly in the night.
Orange and round overhead
Like the night light near my bed.
Flicker, flicker little light
Shining brightly in the night.

Buzz, buzz, yellow bee
Have you any honey?
Yes sir, yes sir.
I sell it for money.
1 jar is a nickel
2 jars are a dime
Come and buy some
    from me anytime.

2. Re-write fairy tales in rhyme.

Little Red in her riding hood
Headed for Grandma's as fast as she could.
The wolf had crumpets and grandma with tea.
Then waited for Red as sweet as can be.

by Leslie Tryon

Three Gruff goats
(With hairy coats)
    Lived on the side of a hill.
They nibbled grass seeds
And tasty green weeds
    Like clover, wild oats, and dill.
A frightful troll
(With a big brown mole)
    Lived under the bridge nearby.
He wouldn't permit
Anyone to cross it
    But the goats decided to try.

51

3. Select a topic. Try to write poems on that topic using several styles.

Topic — Halloween

(Couplet)
> My friend Tom gave me a fright
> When I saw him Halloween night.

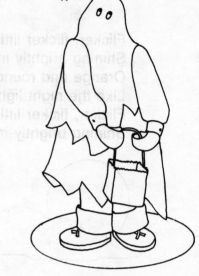

(Cinquain)
> Night
> Quiet darkness
> Children move about
> Shivers and excited giggles
> Halloween

(Haiku)
> A still autumn night
> Excited child creeps about—
> Halloween has come.

4. Describe yourself using your favorite verse form.

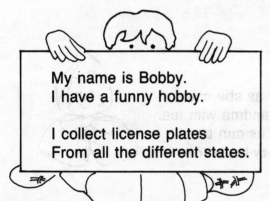

> My name is Bobby.
> I have a funny hobby.
>
> I collect license plates
> From all the different states.

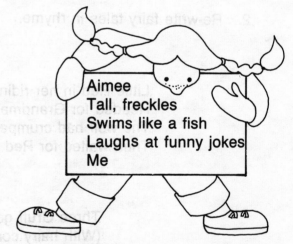

> Aimee
> Tall, freckles
> Swims like a fish
> Laughs at funny jokes
> Me

5. Create an alphabet or counting book in rhyme.

A The letter A
B Rests on hay

While letter B
Floats in the sea.

Five chicks in a nest
Take a little rest.

A swarm of six bees
Flew around the trees.

5
6

And more...

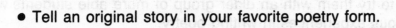

- Tell an original story in your favorite poetry form.

- Re-write the words to your favorite song.

- Make a wish for yourself (or someone else) in rhyme.

- Go for a walk. Create a poem about something you see, feel, hear, smell, or taste.

- Write a riddle in rhyme.

- Create a lovely (or funny) verse for a _____ card.

  Christmas
  Valentine
  Easter
  Birthday
  Congratulations
  I'm Sorry

- Follow a pattern — The _____ is _____
  As _____

  The fog is gray
  As smoke rising high.
  The fog is quiet
  As a cat passing by.

- Start a list of words and sounds you enjoy. See if you can arrange some of the words in your list into an order that creates a poem.

- Write a poem that makes someone laugh out loud.

- Write a poem that shows someone how you feel when you are _____.

sad	angry	lonely
embarrassed	frightened	hurt

And still more...

These poetry forms are too complicated for most elementary level students. You may want to try them with an older group of more able students who have had previous experiences in writing poetry.

Blank verse — Blank verse usually consists of long, unrhymed lines such as unrhymed iambic pentameter. Many of Henry Wadsworth Longfellow's poems are written in blank verse (example — <u>Hiawatha</u>). Beginners need to be careful that they do not have too many end-stopped lines and to vary the placement of pauses from sentence to sentence.

Free verse — Rhythm is the important element in free verse rather than a specific meter form. Walt Whitman is an excellent example of a poet of free verse. More able students can use alliteration, assonance, and even an occasional rhyme to add interest when writing free verse.

Sonnets — A sonnet expresses a single thought, feeling, or mood in fourteen lines. The Shakespearean sonnet is less difficult than other sonnet forms for beginners to attempt. It has fourteen lines of iambic pentameter following this rhyming pattern:

a
b
a
b
c
d
c
d
e
f
e
f
g
g

Remember, these are difficult forms. Be sure to offer plenty of time for re-writing if you have students attempt any of them.

 Writing Poetry With Children

What do I do with all of these poems?

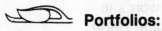

 Portfolios:
Use an art period near the beginning of the school year to create individual portfolios in which to save original poetry. These can be as simple as large manila envelopes decorated with marking pens or crayons. They may be elaborate portfolios made from butcher paper or tagboard decorated with paper collages or block printing.

As the year progresses, each child saves his/her poetry in the portfolio. When you are ready to create newsletters or books, each child will have a nice selection from which to choose. It is exciting for children (and the teacher) to see how much improvement occurs over a period of time.

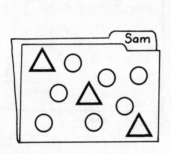 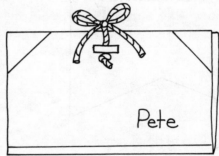

 Display Boards:
If you plan to do a great deal of writing during the school year, you may want to set aside one bulletin board area just for displaying your students' original writings.

Charts and Banners:

Display your students' original poetry on banners or charts. Older students can write and illustrate their own. Younger students may need the teacher's help in printing the words in large enough letters. They can do their own decorations. Hang these in the classroom on a bulletin board or chart rack so that other children can share and enjoy them.

The fog is gray
As smoke rising
    high.
The fog is quiet
As a cat passing by.

Flicker, flicker
little light
Shining brightly
in the night.

Newsletter:

Once a month (quarter, semester, etc.) send home a newsletter containing some of your students' original poetry created during that period. Use the form on page 58 or help your students create their own format.

Our Poetry News

Issue number 2   date December

Aimee
Tall, freckles
Swim like a fish
Laugh at jokes
Me
            Aimee J.

Crocodile
Has teeth
Scaring enemies
Full after his meal
Sleep
            Tara

Upward in flight
Sails my rainbow
      kite.
What a pretty sight
            Troy

Oh, ancient oak tree
how strange, your
    rugged bark felt
to curious hands
            Jo Ellen

The hungry frog
resting on a lily pad
dreams of careless flies
            Danielle

Hamsters
Furry Creatures
Twitching noses,
Loving cozy
    fluffy cotton
Cuddly
            Leslie

Writing Poetry With Children

Program:
Invite parents to a spring program where children recite their own (or classmates) poetry. (Some children may prefer to recite with a group.) This doesn't need to be a complicated process. Children sitting in groups on the stage or on stools can be as effective as elaborate staging and costumes. Punch and cookies afterwards gives everyone a chance to get better acquainted (and to pass around compliments to your young poets).

You may use the invitation form (page 59) and the program form (page 60) or have your students create their own.

 Books:
Bind collections of poems together to keep in your class library center. Children love an opportunity to re-read their own poems and those of their classmates. A variety of binding techniques is shown on pages 61-63.

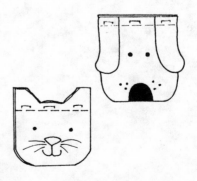

_____

newsletter title

Issue number _____   date _____

_____

proudly
presents

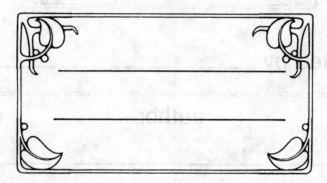

_____

_____

Join us to hear original poetry
written by our class this year.

Time: _____

Place:_____

Please join us!

_____

_____

presented by _____

poem	author	recited by

Making Poetry Books

One of the best ways to motivate your students to write poetry is to provide many opportunities for sharing their finished works. Putting books written and illustrated by your students into a class library is one excellent way for this sharing to take place. You will find students reading and re-reading their own poems as well as those created by their classmates. These books can contain the whole class' efforts to create poems in one style or on one topic or can be individual books containing all of one child's favorites.

Putting a book together:

1. Create pages —

| front cover | title page | poem pages | back cover |

2. Attach poem pages —

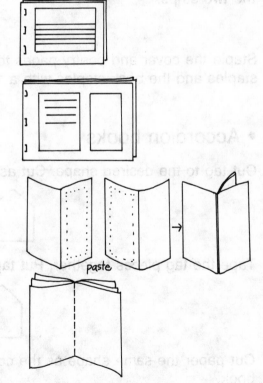

Pages may be stapled together before being put into a cover.

Pages may be glued to a backing of construction paper, then stapled together and put into a cover.

Pages may be folded in half, then glued back-to-back.

Pages may be folded and then stitched down the center. Stitching may be done by machine or by hand with darning needles.

3. Covers —
Covers can be made from many different materials:

mat board   cardboard
construction paper   wallpaper
tag board   cloth

• Quick and easy covers — These covers require little time to create.

a. Staple cover to pages. Cover the staples with a strip of tape.

b. Punch holes through the cover and pages Put together with metal rings. Or tie with shoelaces, yarn, or string.

1. down through end holes

2. up through middle holes

3. tie on top

• Hinged covers

Cut two pieces of tag, cardboard, etc. slightly larger than the poetry pages.

Cut 1/2" strip from the left-hand side of the front cover.

Tape the strips together on the inside. Leave an 1/8" space open between the two strips.

Staple the cover and poetry pages together. Cover the front hinge and staples and the back staples with a 1 1/2" piece of tape.

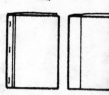

• Accordion books

Cut tag to the desired shape. Cut as many pieces as you need.

Tape the tag pieces together. Put tape front and back.

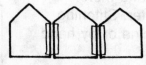

Cut paper the same shape as the cover. Write poems and glue into the book.

• Cloth covers

Cut two pieces of cardboard slightly larger than the poetry pages.

Place the cardboard on a piece of cloth 1 to 1 1/2'' larger than the cover. Leave a small space in between the cover pieces.

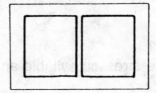

Miter the corners of the fabric.

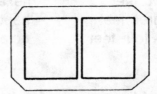

Place diluted white glue on the cloth and fold over the cover. (Place waxed paper inside the book and place a heavy object on top of the cover as it dries.)

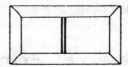

Poetry pages should be cut almost the length of the cover. Stitch 46 pages together down the center with a darning needle and thread or on a sewing machine.

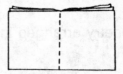

Leave the first and last pages empty to serve as end pages. Write and illustrate the poems. Paste the end papers to the cover to complete the book. (Place waxed paper between the end papers and the poetry pages while the glue is drying.)

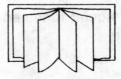

Poetry Terms

Accent — the stronger tone of voice that is given to certain syllables or words.

Feet — a foot consists of one stressed syllable and one or two unstressed syllables.

monometer — one foot	pentameter — five feet
dimeter — two feet	hexameter — six feet
trimeter — three feet	heptameter — seven feet
tetrameter — four feet	octometer — eight feet

Meter — the rhythm pattern of lines in a poem. It is the arrangement of accents in a line of poetry.

Poem — a form of writing in verse. While many poems consist of lines that rhyme, rhyming is not necessary to create a poem.

Rhyme — to sound alike in the last part. (Example: verse — purse, snow — below, bent — dent.)

Rhythm — a regular repetition of a beat or accent.

Stanza — a group of lines of poetry arranged in a specific order. (A verse of a poem.)

Syllable — a word or part of a word pronounced as one unit. A syllable usually consists of a vowel alone or a vowel with one or more consonants.

Verse — lines of words with a regular repeated accent which often rhyme. (A group of lines of poetry.)

64   Writing Poetry With Children